Tidepool & Reef
Marinelife Guide
to the Pacific Northwest Coast

Rick M. Harbo

hancock

house

ISBN 0-88839-039-4
Copyright © 1980 Rick M. Harbo

Second Printing 1984

Canadian Cataloguing in Publication Data

Harbo, Rick M., 1949-
  Tidepool and Reef

(Natural history series)
Bibliography: p.
ISBN 0-88839-052-1

1. Marine fauna - Northwest coast of North
America. 2. Interstitial fauna - Northwest
coast of North America. 3. Seashore biology -
Northwest coast of North America. I. Title.
II. Series: Natural history series (North
Vancouver, B.C.)

QH95.3.H37   591.92'53   C80-091146-6

Printed in Canada by Friesen Printers

Published simultaneously in Canada and the United States by

HANCOCK HOUSE PUBLISHERS LTD.
19313 Zero Ave., Surrey, B.C. V3S 5J9

HANCOCK HOUSE PUBLISHERS INC.
1431 Harrison Avenue, Blaine, WA 98230

Table Of Contents

Page

Acknowledgements, Photo Credits.................. 4
Bibliography... 4
Introduction 5

I. Animals—*invertebrates and vertebrates*
Phylum Porifera
Sponges 6
Phylum Coelenterata
Hydroids... 8
Hydrocorals.. 10
Sea Pens 11
Soft Corals & Cup Corals......................... 12
Anemones 13
Jellyfish (Medusae)................................ 16
Phylum Platyhelminthes
Flatworms... 18
Phylum Nemertea
Ribbon Worms..................................... 18
Phylum Bryozoa
Bryozoans 20
Phylum Brachiopoda
Lampshells.. 21
Phylum Mollusca
Chitons 21
Snails 22
Limpets 24
Sea Slugs or Nudibranches 25
Bivalves... 30
Octopus and Squid 33
Phylum Arthropoda
Barnacles 34
Shrimp and Amphipods........................... 35
Crabs 36
Phylum Echinodermata
Sea Stars 40
Sea Cucumbers 44
Sand Dollars and Sea Urchins 45
Phylum Chordata
Sea Squirts and Tunicates 46
Cartilaginous Fishes............................... 48
Bony Fishes 48
    Sculpins 48
    Rockfishes..................................... 49
    Perch.. 51
    Greenlings 51
    Pricklebacks, Warbonnets & Wolf-eels 52
    Flatfishs 52
II. Plants
Green Seaweed 53
Brown Seaweed 53
Red Seaweed 54
Seed Plants 55
Index... 56

Acknowledgements

I would like to thank my diving buddies, and particularly Neil McDaniel and Lou Lehmann for the experiences shared photographing marine life.

I would also like to thank Margaret Thompson for typing the manuscript and my wife, Heather, for her assistance in editing and proofreading.

Photo Credits

P.33 Opalescent squid by Ron Church.

Bibliography

Hart, J.L. *Pacific Fishes of Canada*. Ottawa: Fisheries Research Board of Canada. Bulletin 180, 1973.

Kozloff, E.N. *Seashore Life of Puget Sound, the Strait of Georgia and the San Juan Archipelago*. Seattle. University of Washington Press. 1973.

Scagel, R.F. *Guide to Common Seaweeds of British Columbia*. Handbook No.27, Victoria: British Columbia Provincial Museum. 1971.

Snively, G. 1978.*Exploring the Seashore in British Columbia Washington and Oregon. A guide to Shorebirds and Intertidal Plants and Animals*. Vancouver: Gordon Soules Book Publishers. 1978.

Introduction

Tidepool and Reef is intended as a field guide for beach explorers, skindivers and scuba divers. I have given a photograph and brief description for each common, and many not so commonly found species of plants and animals-its size, shape, color and habitat. Some additional characteristicsmay also be included in the general description of the group of organisms.

Distribution Of Animals And Plants

The guide is organized by similar groups of animals and plants rather than by habitats. The geographical distribution of most of the plants and animals is from central California to Alaska including Oregon, Washington and British Columbia.

The accompanying sketch indicates the intertidal and subtidal zones, down to a depth of 36 m, the recognized limit of sport diving. A precise description of an organism's habitat is often difficult. The distribution depends on very local physical characteristics such as temperature, wave action, tidal height, currents, and the type of substrate, for example, rock, mud, sand. Salinity, freshwater runoff, organic nutrients, pollution and other chemical factors also play an important role in survival.

Biological factors cannot be ignored. There are dynamic prey-predator relationships that control populations of organisms. In addition, physical and chemical factors are important in reproduction and the survival of the eggs and larvae.

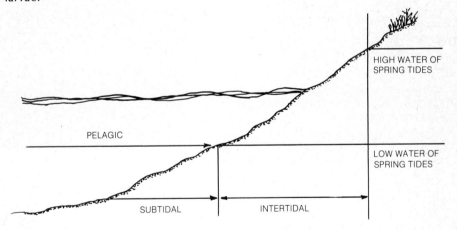

HIGH WATER OF SPRING TIDES

PELAGIC

LOW WATER OF SPRING TIDES

SUBTIDAL   INTERTIDAL

Collecting

Please capture the seashore with your camera; leave it for others to see. If you are harvesting.food, consult your local fisheries department (state, provincial or federal) forsize and sex restrictions, bag limits, possession limits, and area and seasonal closures. Watch for posted notices of shellfish contamination by red tides or pollution. Take only what you can use.

Please return overturned rocks to their original positions and fill in any holes that have been dug.

Above all enjoy the seashore.

Phylum Porifera:

These are animals but exhibit little detectable movement. Cells are organized around a system of pores, canals and chambers. Form soft and spongy encrusting mats; baselike, tubelike, or with erect, branching growths. Found on or under rocks, in crevices and on floats and pilings.

Sponges

Crumb Of Bread Sponge: *Halichondria panicea:*

Often yellow, orange to green color. Encrusting to 6 mm thick. Raised large volcano -like pores or "oscula". Often found on floats.

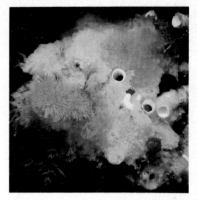

◄Encrusting Sponge:

Haliclona permollis:

Often purple. Raised oscula. On rocks at low tide.

Tube Sponge:

Leucosolenia eleanor: ►

Small mass of branching tubes of one mm diameter. Often found on floats and in protected waters.

Yellow Boring Sponge:

Cliona celata:

Small, yellow patches showing at surface. Decomposed shells of mollusks (here a scallop) and barnacles. ▼

Red Sponge:

Ophlitaspongia pennata: ►

Red, thin encrusting sponge. Red nudibranch, *Rostanga pulchra,* often associated with this sponge. Found in narrow crevices and under rocks.

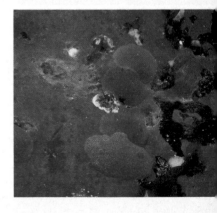

White Encrusting Sponge:
Adocia mollis:
Large encrusting clumps, prominent oscula.
Often found on floats and pilings.

Rough Encrusting Sponge:
Myxilla incrustans:
Often raised oscula to six mm diameter.
Rough texture, yellow to yellow-brown. Often
found on shells of swimming scallops.

Smooth Encrusting Sponge: *Mycale adhaerens:*
Oscula to four mm diameter. Smooth texture,
light brown to violet. Found regularly on
shells of swimming scallops.▼

Hermit Crab Sponge:
Suberites domuncula:
Grows on shells inhabited by hermit crabs;
eventually dissolves the shell. Instead of
finding larger shells as the crab grows, it can
make the sponge its permanent home.

Bristly Vase Sponge:
Leucandra heathi:
Bristly sponge to 25 cm. high, with long guard
bristles at the top opening, the "oscula". Found
on rocks and floats.

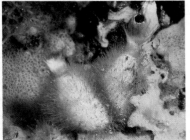

Cloud Sponge:
Aphrocallistes vastus:
Glass sponge, massive, erect branching
growths which provide shelter for a variety of
creatures. Strictly subtidal.

Phylum Coelenterata:

"Sac" body with many tentacles and stinging cells. Includes hydroids, corals, seapens, anemones and jellyfish. No edible species.

Hydroids

(Plylum Coelenterata): Solitary or bushy growths. Have delicate, feeding tentacles which are often preyed upon by nudibranchs. Attached to rocks, shells and floats in the lower subtidal zone.

◄ Orange Hydroid:

Garveia annulata: Small polyps, form bright, orange, bushy clusters to 15 cm high. Found on rocks, floats, and on stalks of kelp. Abundant in winter and spring months.

Hedgehog Hydroid: ►

Hydractinia milleri: Pink, fuzzy masses to 2.5 cm. Found on hermit crab shells. Forms clusters on rocks.

Pink Mouth Hydroid:

Tubularia crocea: Clusters of hydroids up to 15 cm. Brown straw-like stems with delicate pink and red polyps. Found on wharf pilings, floats, rocks and boat bottoms. ▼

Pink Mouth Hydroid: ▲

Tubularia marina: Common, orange-pink polyp on solitary slender stalk to 8 cm. Two sets of tentacles. Found on rocks and floats.

◄ Sea Fir:

Abietinaria sp.: To 15 cm. Main stem and branches form firm feather-like pattern with polyps on both sides of the branches. Found on rocks.

Ostrich Plume Hydroid: ►

Aglaophenia struthionides: To 15 cm. Firm texture, feather-like pattern. Individual feeding polyps only on one side of each branch. Found on rocks.

Hydrocorals:

*(Phylum Coelenterata):*Not well-known, but are moderately common in shallow, subtidal areas.

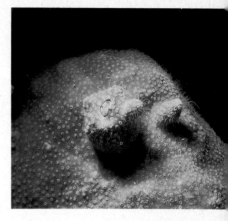

Encrusting Hydrocorals: ►

Allopora petrograpta: Large, thin encrusting patches, often confused with corraline algae. Vivid purple or pink. Pattern of small holes harbours polyps. Found on intertidal and subtidal rocks.

Branching Hydrocorals:

Three species are illustrated. They are all attached to subtidal rocks.

◄ Allopora venusta:

Thickly branching. Rose-pink or faded violet with tips of branch lacking pigment. Extensive colonies.

Allopora verilli:

Calacreous mass of thickly branching colonies to 10 cm diameter Salmon-pink color.   ►

Allopora sp.:

To 10 cm diameter. Mass of thick branches. Bright pink. Prominent holes harbour small polyps.▼

Sea Pens

(Phylum Coelenterata): Tall, branching feather-like colonies with numerous polyps on the branches. Each polyp has eight tentacles. Found in subtidal mud or sand.

Orange Sea Pen:

Ptilosarcus gurneyi: To one m tall. Orange, feather-like colony. Numerous tentacles along the branches are shown in close-up.

White Sea Pen:

Virgularia tuberculata: Slender, reaching only 20 cm in height. Whole colony can retract into soft mud. Often found in association with sea whips.

Sea Whip:

Osteocella septentrionalis: To 2.5 m tall. Largest sea pen known. Found at depths of 20 m or deeper.

Soft Corals

Phylum Coelenterata
Soft branching masses. Colonies of
polyps with eight tentacles.

Soft Coral: ▶

Gersemia rubiformis: Height to 10 cm.
Branching mass with polyps having eight
tentacles, shown expanded and retracted.
Variable in color from pale orange to red.
Found on rocks at lowest tides and subtidally
in current-swept areas. ▼

Cup Corals *Phylum Coelenterata*

Transparent tentacles originating from
a single calcareous cup.

Orange Cup Coral: *Balanophyllia elegans:*

Solitary calcareous cup to two cm. Bright
orange polyps with short transparent tentacles.
Found on subtidal rocks, occasionally
intertidal.
▼

◀ **Tan Cup Coral:** *Caryophyllia alaskensis:*
Solitary cup to three cm. Tan colored polyps
with long, transparent tentacles. Found on
subtidal rocks.

Anemones:

Phylum Coelenterata:
"Flower-like" animals sometime variable in color. Found in tidepools, on rocks, floats and pilings, and in sediments. Many are found in the lower intertidal zone, but most are subtidal. Not edible.

Plumose Anemones: *Metridium senile:* ►
Height to 90 cm. White, orange or brown color. Many very slender tentacles. Common on wharves, pilings, and rocks. Tentacles will retract into base.

Painted Tealia: *Tealia crassicornis:*
Common, to 25 cm. in diameter and height. Column color is often mottled red and green but may be orange, brown or cream. Short tentacles, usually white with a typically rose colored mid-band. ◄

Buried Tealia: *Tealia coriacea:*
Diameter of red beaded column to 15 cm. Short, blunt, banded tentacles. Pale pink to green. Found buried to disc in sand-shell sediments. ▼

White-Spotted Tealia: *Tealia lofotensis:*
To 15 cm. Scarlet column with longitudinal ►
rows of white spots. Tentacles are yellowish at base with pink tips. Found on exposed shores.

Fish-Eating Tealia: *Tealia piscivora:*
◄ Diameter to 25 cm. smooth maroon column with many white or pink tentacles-not banded. Captures and eats small fish. Found subtidally on open coast.

Giant Green Anemone
Anthopleura xanthogrammica:

Diameter to 25 cm. Drab olive-brown column. Green tentacles are colored by symbiotic algae. Commonly found in tidepools on exposed shores.

Aggregate Anemone
◄*Anthopleura elegantissima:*

Beaded column from three cm. diameter to eight cm. Pale tentacles with pink to purple tips have symbiotic algae. Found in tidepools and covering intertidal rocks.

Buried Green Anemone:
Anthopleura artemisia:

Diameter to ten cm. Long and slender; banded tentacles have symbiotic algae. Found buried to disc in sand-shell sediments.

▼

◄**Brooding Anemone:** *Epiactis prolifera:*
Diameter to eight cm. Column vertically striped with radiating white lines on oral disc. Broods young on column. Color is variable: orange, green or pink. Commonly found on eelgrass and rocks.

Strawberry Anemone:
Corynactis californica: ➤

Diameter to two cm. Pale to brilliant red. Short tentacles end in white club. Found on rocks in current-swept areas.

Zoanthids *Epizoanthus scotinus:*

Diameter to two cm. Forms orange colonies blanketing rocks. ▼

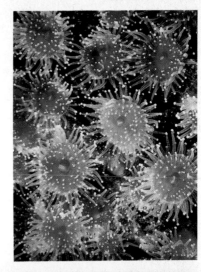

Swimming Anemone: ▲
Stomphia didemon:

Diameter to 12 cm. Orange column with white banded tentacles. Will release from bottom and swim in response to touch of the leather sea star. Found on subtidal rocks.

▲
Crimson Anemone: *Cribrinopsis fernaldi:*

Diameter and column to 20 cm. Variable in color: white, pink or crimson. Has long slender tentacles with "varicose" pattern. Found on subtidal rocks.

Tube-Dwelling Anemone:
Pachycerianthus fimbriatus: ➤

Mucous-like tube to four cm. diameter harbours this anemone. Short inner tentacles and long outer tentacles may be colorless, striped or port-wine color. Animal can retract quickly down the tube, which projects out of the mud bottom.

Jellyfish or Medusae:

Phylum Coelenterata:
Bell-shaped animals with trailing tentacles.

Hydrozoan Medusae:

Small jellyfish, less than ten cm. are often juvenile stages of hydroids

Clinging Jellyfish: *Gonionemus vertens:* ➤
Diameter to three cm. Cross-shaped sex
organs in dome. Clings to kelp or eelgrass by
adhesive pads on tentacles. Abundant in
summer.

Sail Jellyfish: *Velella velella:*
"By the wind sailors", to ten cm. in dia. with
a small transparent sail. Actually a colonial
hydroid often washed ashore ⬆

Water Jellyfish: *Aequorea aequorea:*
Fifty-nine to ten cm. diameter. Numerous radial
canals. Many tentacles. Luminescent at night.
▼

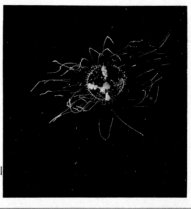

Scyphozoan Medusae:

"True" jellyfish are usually larger jellyfish
10 cm. or greater, and differ somewhat in
structure from hydromedusae.

◄**Moon Jellyfish:** *Aurelia aurita:*
Ten to 15 cm. across bell. Eight equal
marginal lobes, four horseshoe-shaped
gonads.

Sea Blubber: *Cyanea capillata:* ➤
To 50 cm. or more across bell. Tentacles,
often longer than 3 m, give a rash. Yellowish-
brown color. Abundant in late summer.

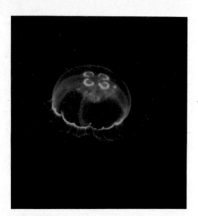

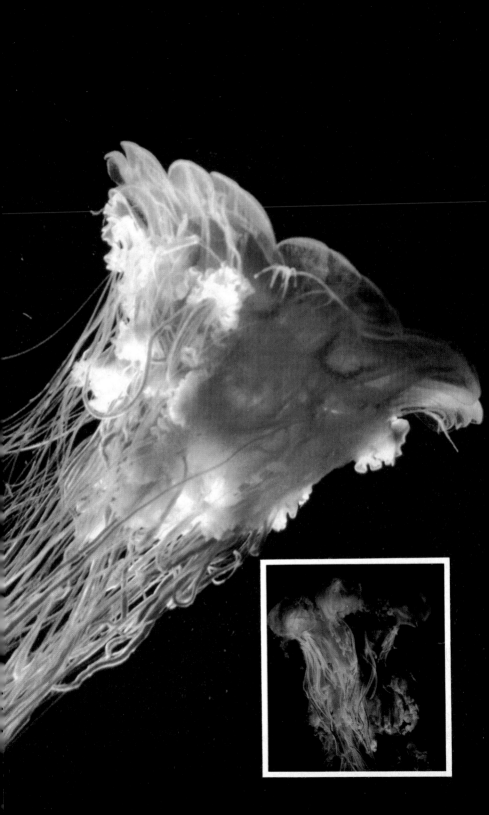

Phylum Platyhelminthes:

Flatworms

Length to five cm. Thin, flattened, oval worms that may be parasitic or free-living. Tan to brown in color, often spotted. Found in mussel beds and under rocks. Difficult to identify in the field. ➤

Phylum Nemertea:

From less than one cm. to six cm. Clearly not segmented. Variety of colors. Have long tubular proboscis often with stylet and poison sac. Often under intertidal rocks or in clumps of mussels.

Ribbon Worms

Green And Yellow Ribbon Worm:
Emplectonema gracile:

To 30 cm. long. Dark green dorsal, whitish or yellow ventral. Found under intertidal rocks and in mussel beds.

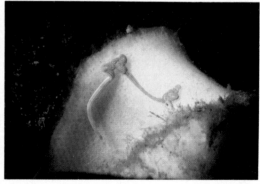

Primitive Ribbon Worm: *Tubulanus* ▲ *polymorphus:*

To one m long. Orange in color.

Lined Ribbon Worm: *Tubulanus sexlineatus:*

To 50 cm. Chocolate brown interrupted by evenly spaced white rings or five of six longitudinal white lines. Found under rocks or on floats.

Phylum Annelida:

Segmented worms to 50 cm. Free-living or in a parchment-like or calcareous tube.

Segmented Worms

Calcareous Tube Worm: *Serpula* ►
vermicularis:

Height to 10 cm. Segmented body. Red and white tentacles retract into a coiled calcareous tube to form a conical stopper. Found on intertidal rocks and floats.

◄ Feather Duster Worm: *Eudistylia*
vancouveri:

To 45 cm. Dark brown parchment-like tube. Maroon and green striped, feathery tentacles up to eight cm. diameter. No stopper. Found on pilings and rocks.

Cemented Tube Worm: *Dodecaceria* ►
fewkesi:

Clumps to 50 cm of hard, calcareous tubes, projecting from a concreted base. Found on rocks or shells in shallows.

Scaleworms: *Halosydna brevisetosa:* ▲

To 5 cm. Free-living. Grey or brownish-grey with cross bands. Eighteen pairs of scales. Often found in commensal relationships with starfish and keyhole limpets.

Large Mussel Worms: *Nereis vexillosa:* ►

To 20 cm. in length. Free-swimming. Iridescent greenish brown. Divided into more than 100 segments, each has paddle-like feet. Found in mussel beds.

Phylum Bryozoa

Often overlooked or mistaken for hydroids. Form colonies of microscopic animals in box-like compartments, as thin crusty patches, branching, lacy or bushy growths on rocks, floats, pilings and kelp. Not edible.

Bryozoans

Staghorn Bryozoan "False Coral":

Heteropora pacifica: ➤

Clumps to 4.5 cm. Resembles coral. Blunt, forked and rounded branches. Found on shallow rocks.

Lacy Bryozoan: *Phidolopora pacifica:*

Colony like a ruffled lacy network. White to orange. Calcareous, inflexible spiral. Found in shallows.

Spiral Bryozoan: *Bugula sp.:*

To 25 cm. Lacy, spiral pattern of branches. Found in shallows, often on floats. ▼

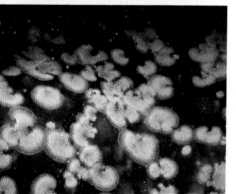

Kelp Encrusting Bryozoan:

Membranipora membranacea:

Two to ten cm. Thin, nearly circular, silver patches of small rectangles. Common on kelp in late spring or summer.

Orange Encrusting Bryozoan:

Schizoporella bicornis:

Thicker and less regular than *Membranipora*. Dingy orange color. Found all seasons. Common on rocks, shells of mussels and barnacles.

Phylum Brachiopoda

Often mistaken for a bivalve mollusc. Two shells with a short flexible stalk for attachment. Resemble ancient oil lamps hence, lampshells. Paired feeding structure inside shell captures food particles.

Lampshells   *Terebratalia transversa:*   ▶

Diameter to three cm. Shells may be smooth or strongly ribbed. Where the shells are hinged, there is a hole for the stalk. Forward lip of lower shell has a distinct "dent". Sometimes found intertidally in protected waters or subtidally on more exposed shores.

Phylum Mollusca:

Abundant, conspicuous, soft-bodied animals. Most have calcareous shells and a muscular foot for "creeping" locomotion. Many have a rasp-like tongue for scraping algae. Includes chitons, snails, sea slugs, clams, oysters, musssels, squids and octopuses. Many are edible.

Chitons

Eight overlapping plates embedded in a flattened oval body. Feed by scraping algae with a toothlike *"radula"*. Adhere tightly to intertidal and subtidal rocks and shells.

Giant Gumboot Chiton: *Cryptochiton stelleri:*   ▶

To 35 cm. Largest chiton in the world. No valves (plates) showing. Completely covered by thick gritty girdle. Brown-red. Commonly hosts a scale worm on the underside. Often found intertidally.

Lined Chiton: *Tonicella lineata:*

To five cm. Brightly colored with dark zigzagging lines over light background of yellow, orange, pink, orchid, and lavender. Often found grazing on coralline algae, *Lithothamnion.*   ▶

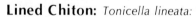

Black Leather Chiton: *Katharina tunicata:* ▼

To seven cm. Black girdle almost covers valves. Grazes on algae that coats the rocks.

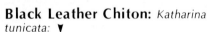

Mossy Chiton: *Mopalia muscosa:*   ▶

To eight cm. Margin or "girdle" has hairs and bristles. Sometimes encrusted with barnacles or other organisms.

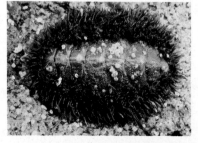

Snails: *Phylum Mollusca:*

A group of animals with unsegmented bodies encased in a single, spiral, calcareous shell. Most are edible.

Northern Abalone:
Haliotis kamtschatkana: ➤

To 17 cm. Flattened snail with row of holes along margin of shell. Edible, harvested commercially.Ranges from Alaska to central California. Found at lowest tides.

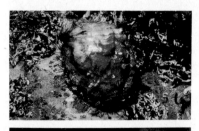

Moon Snail: *Polinices lewisii:*

To 12 cm. Most massive intertidal snail. ➤ Mantle covers all of shell. Often submerged in sand, feeding on bivalves. Edible. Egg case shown. ➤

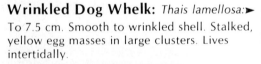

▼

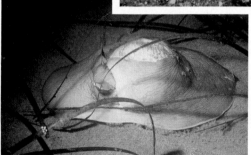

Wrinkled Dog Whelk: *Thais lamellosa:*➤
To 7.5 cm. Smooth to wrinkled shell. Stalked, yellow egg masses in large clusters. Lives intertidally.

Ribbed Whelk: *Thais emarginata:*
To 2.5 cm. short and plump. Strongly developed spiral ribs. Variable color: green. black, brown or yellow often with white bands. Feeds on barnacles.

Leafy Hornmouth: *Ceratostoma foliatum:*
To eight cm. Shell has extensive frills and a big tooth at the tapering end. Lays yellow egg cases on subtidal rocks. ➤

Ringed Top Snail: *Calliostoma annulatum:*

Height to three cm. Purplish tints on yellowish conical shell. Snail is bright orange. Usually subtidal.

Blue Top Snail: *Calliostoma ligatum:* ➤

To three cm, height is slightly greater than width. Shaped like a top, with brick red stripes that follow the whorls.

◄ **Black Turban Snail:** *Tegula funebralis:*

Height to three cm. Low cone of four, rounded whorls. Purplish-black with pearly interior. Common among rocks in tidepools .

Spindle Whelk: *Searlesia dira:*

Height to 3.5 cm. Conspicuous spiral threads. Dark-brownish gray. Found on intertidal and subtidal rocks. ▼

Hairy or Oregon Triton: *Fusitriton oregonensis:*

To 12 cm. Largest snail found in our region. Eggs are laid in translucent egg cases that form a spiral pattern. Usually subtidal. ▼

Mudflat Snail: *Batillaria attramentaria* ➤

Height to three cm. Eight or nine whorls. Greyish color with darker-brown "beads". Found on intertidal mudflats.

Limpets:

Single shell does not spiral but is conical or cap-shaped, sometimes irregular. Feeds on algae. Although small, most are edible. All are found intertidally and on floats.

Keyhole Limpet: *Diodora aspera:*
To five cm. Large ribbed shell with hole at the apex. Often host a scale worm. Found at the lowest tide levels.

Whitecap Limpet: *Acmaea mitra:*

To three cm. diameter. Heavy shell, white inside and out. Often overgrown by pink coralline algae, on which this species feeds. Found intertidally.

Plate Limpet: *Notoacmea scutum:*

To four cm. diameter. Flat, smooth shell. Grey or olive with lighter spots or streaks. Found intertidally.

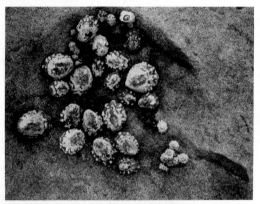

Finger Limpet: *Collisella digitalis:*

To 2.5 cm. diameter. Hooked shell with strong ribs and scalloped margin. Brown or greyish, with dark zigzag markings. Found on intertidal rocks on exposed shores.

Speckled Limpet: *Notoacmea persona:*
To four cm. Small white dots on top, with larger white spots on brown base of shell.

Nudibranchs: *Phylum Mollusca:*

Fat, slug-like bodies, without shells. Often have bumps or finger-like processes ("*cerata*") and a pair of tentacles called "*rhinophores*" that are chemosensory. Some have delicate plume-like gills. Nudibranchs eat sponges, hydroids and many other animals. Some are found intertidally but most are subtidal.

Brown Spotted Nudibranch: *Diaulula sandiegensis:*

Length to eight cm. Body white to dusky grey with scattered brown spots often with lighter rings. Has retractable, plume-like gills. Eats intertidal and subtidal sponges. Found subtidally and intertidally.

Sea Lemon: *Anisodoris nobilis:*

To eight cm. Yellow to orange with black spots between bumps (tubercles). Has mucous and an odor. Has retractable plume-like gills.

Sea Lemon: *Archidoris montereyensis:*

To eight cm. Lemon-yellow to greenish-yellow; rarely orange. Has little mucous and no odor. Has retractable plume-like gills. Sometimes found on floats.

Brown Barnacle Nudibranch:

Onchidoris bilamellata:

To three cm. Brown coloration concentrated in bands. Lays eggs in extensive white ribbons. Feeds exclusively on intertidal barnacles. Has plume-like retractable gills.

Sea Lemon:

Aldisa sanguinea cooperi:

To six cm. Yellow to orange with black spots along midline. Has retractable plume-like gills.

Common Orange Spotted Nudibranch: *Triopha catilinae :* ►

To seven cm. White body with orange bumpy processes. Orange on the tips of the plume-like gills.

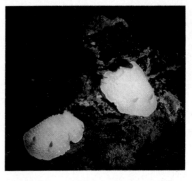

Orange Spotted Nudibranch: *Laila cockerelli:*

To three cm. Orange on the tips of long fleshy projections. No spots. Small, white plume-like gills. Uncommon.

▼

Common Yellow-Margin Nudibranch: *Cadlina luteomarginata:*

Broad, flat body. White with low, yellow bumps and yellow margin. Retractable plume-like gills. Common on rocky shores. ▼

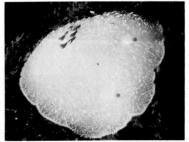

Adalaria sp.:

To two cm. White body with many bumps. Has retractable plume-like gills. Lays eggs in white ribbons, often on kelp.

▼

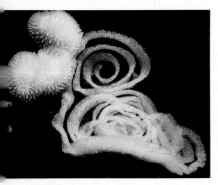

Nanaimo Nudibranch: *Acanthodoris nanaimoensis:* ▼

To four cm. Another nudibranch with a yellow margin and long slender projections but this one has wine-brown markings on the plume-like gills and the rhinophores.

Acanthodoris hudsoni: ►

To four cm. Has yellow margin, but with long slender projections. Retractable plume-like gills.

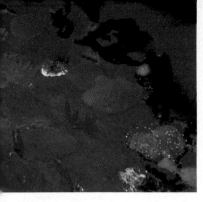

Red Nudibranch: *Rostanga pulchra:*
To two cm. Red-orange. Retractable plume-like gills. Commonly feeds on intertidal red sponge.

White Nudibranch: *Archidoris odhneri:*
To eight cm. Plump, white body with many small bumps. Has retractable plume-like gills. Often observed feeding on sponges.

▼

Coryphella salmonacea:

To five cm. Body and cerata cream colored. Lays eggs in small, coiled, spiral ribbons.

▼

Coryphella rufibranchialis:

To two cm. White body with red cerata tipped with white. Feeds on hydroids.

▼

Coryphella trilineata: ▲

To three cm. Three longitudinal white lines on body. Red cerata with white tips. Found feeding on hydroids.

Coryphella fusca: ▲

To six cm. Dark cerata with white tips. Also observed eating hydroids.

Opalescent Nudibranch: *Hermissenda crassicornis:*

To five cm. Long projections—"cerata"—with white lines and orange tips. Orange band and irridescent blue lines on body. Very common in eelgrass and on rocky shores.

Giant Nudibranch: *Dendronotus iris:* ▲

To 30 cm. Large slug-like body, usually white or colorless, sometimes orange. Has many large branching cerata. Found on mud-sand bottoms, feeding on tube dwelling anemones.

Tritonia diomedea:

To 35 cm. Long, broad body. Pink with tufts of gills around the margin. Observed feeding on white sea pens.

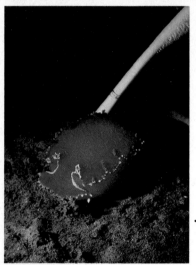

Orange Peel Nudibranch: *Tochuina tetraquetra:*

To 25 cm. Thick body is apricot to orange with white gill tufts on the margin. Feeds on hydroids and the soft coral, *Gersemia.*

▼

Tritonia festiva:

To seven cm. Long, slender body with white, irregular lines. White gill tufts. Also observed feeding on hydroids and soft coral. ▼

Dendronotus diversicolor:

To ten cm. Long slender body with four or five rows of branching cerata. Variable in color. (see photographs) Tips of cerata may be orange or white.

Hooded Nudibranch: *Melibe leonina:*

To seven cm. Unusual looking - a large oval hood with marginal tentacles and 4 to 6 pairs of paddle-shaped appendages (cerata). Colorless and transparent. Found on eelgrass and algae.

Alabaster Nudibranch: *Dirona albolineata:*

To six cm. Translucent body with white lines on edges of both the bulbous cerata and the margin. Often observed browsing on bryozoans. Very common.

Orange Nudibranch: *Dirona aurantia:* ➤

To seven cm. Orange body with white splotches and white lines on edge of cerata.

Striped Nudibranch: *Armina californica:*

To seven cm. Brown with white longitudal ridges. Feeds on sea pens. (Photo close-up shows *Armina* on a sea pen).

Bubble Shell: *Haminoea virescens:*

To two cm. Slug-like body but with an internal shell visible (hence it is not a nudibranch). Brownish, with light and dark mottling. Commonly found on eelgrass.

Bivalves: *Phylum Mollusca:*

Includes common clams, oysters and mussels. Two flattened oval shells are hinged together and held by one or two large muscles. The shells vary in size, shape, sculpturing, and color. Bivalves are found in sand and mud, or attached to rocks or pilings. Some bore into wood or rock.

Warning! Beware of red tides causing paralytic shellfish poisoning (PSP) and of areas contaminated by pollution. Consult local authorities for area and seasonal closures, size restrictions, bag limits and possession limit.

◄ Shipworm: *Bankia setacea:*

To one m in length. Body worm-like with reduced shells. Siphons often extended. Found only boring in wood. Also known as Teredos

Pacific Oyster: *Crassostrea gigas:*

To 30 cm. Shell rough and frilled. Introduced from Japan for commercial fishery. The young "spat" prefer to settle on shells of the adult oyster. Found intertidally in protected waters. ▼

Purple-Hinged Scallop: *Hinnites* ▲ *giganteus:*

Diameter to 25 cm. Age to 15 years or older. Purple-hinged, circular shell, strongly ribbed , usually heavily encrusted with various organisms. Shell is often riddled by boring sponge. Large circular, edible muscle holds shell together. Free-swimming juvenile cements to subtidal rocks.

Pacific Pink Scallop: *Chlamys rubida:* ►

To eight cm. Smooth radial ridges on shell. Sponge usually found on shell. Not as common as *C. hastata hericia.*

Pacific Pink Scallop: *Chlamys hastata* ► *hericia:*

To ten cm. Swimming scallop. Spiny radial ridges on shell. Shells usually covered with sponge. Small muscle is edible. Often harvested by divers.

Bay or Blue Mussel: *Mytilus edulis:* ➤

To five cm. Smooth black, blue or brown shell. Very common intertidally and on floats in protected waters.

California Mussel: *Mytilus californianus:*

To 25 cm. long. Shell has prominent ridges. Bright orange flesh. Beds of mussels are common in intertidal areas on open coast exposed shores. Edible but beware of PSP and pollution. ➤

Northwest Ugly Clam: *Entodesma sax-*▲ *icola:*

To 15 cm. Gaping shell with siphons. External surface covered with thick olive-brown epidermis. Found in crevices among rocks.

Geoduck Clam: *Panope generosa:* ➤

Shell to 20 cm. Average two lbs. or more. Largest burrowing clam in world. Immense siphon. Shell gapes widely. Buried one m deep in sand-mud with siphons protruding Harvested commercially by divers Found subtidally and on lowest tides.
▼

Horse Clam: *Tresus capax:*

To 20 cm. Also has large wrinkled siphon that can be retracted almost completely into shell. Buried to 0.5 m in gravel beach. Protruding siphons have inner fringe of tentacles. ▼

32 Bivalves

Heart Cockle: *Clinocardium nuttallii:* ➤
To ten cm. Strong, radiating ribs. Tan to brown. Often mottled. Found intertidally in sand and mud.

Native Littleneck Clam: *Protothaca staminea:*

To six cm. Radiating and concentric ridges. Found intertidally buried close to surface in gravel mixed with sand and mud. Common edible clam.

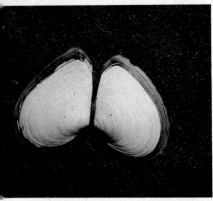

Bent Nose Clam: *Macoma nasuta:*
To five cm. Buried near surface in muddy sand. Shells bend sharply.

Butter Clam: *Saxidomus giganteus:*
To ten cm. Thick, white shell with concentric lines or grooves. Found intertidally in gravel beaches. Popular edible clam.
▼

Razor Clam: *Siliqua patula:* ➤
To 15 cm. Long, thin, polished shell. Brown to yellowish brown. Close to surface, but a fast digger. At lowest tides on surf-beaten sandy beaches. Harvested commercially. Delicious.

Octopus And Squid: *Phylum Mollusca:*

Highly developed mulluscs. Squid have a soft internal "shell" but a shell is absent in the octopus.

◄ Stubby Squid: *Rossia pacifica:*

Short, rounded body to four cm. with small semi-circular fins. Eight short arms and two shorter tentacles. Found subtidally on rocky or sandy bottoms

Opalescent Squid: *Loligo opalescens:* ▲

Rounded, elongated body to 15 cm. with prominent fins. Eight arms and two shorter tentacles. Internal shell or "pen". Lives in groups, free-swimming in open water. Congregates and spawns subtidally along protected shores.

Pacific Octopus:

Octopus dofleini:

To 20 kg. or more. Length to two m. Oval body with eight arms of equal length. Largest octopus in the world. A parrot-like beak. Can change color rapidly. Found on sandy and rocky bottoms, often in dens and occasionally in tidepools. ►

34

Phylum Arthropoda:

Largest number of species and individuals. Has hard, protective outer skeleton and paired, jointed appendages. Varied forms include barnacles, shrimps, crabs, lobsters, amphipods, and many others.

Barnacles:

The "shell" is comprised of overlapping plates and the opening at the top is closed by muscles moving plates. The barnacle "kicks" out legs to capture food. Barnacles may have a tough, flexible stalk or the shell may be cemented directly to objects.

Acorn Barnacle: *Balanus glandula:* ▲
Diameter to 1.5 cm. White. Grow tall when crowded. Very common, small intertidal barnacle on rocks and pilings.

Thatched Barnacle: *Balanus cariosus:*◀
Diameter to five cm. Prominent ridges on shell plates. Not found where there is freshwater input. Common on intertidal rocks, often on floats and pilings.

Goose Barnacle: *Pollicipes polymerus:*▶
Length to eight cm. Tough flexible stalk, topped with five large plates and numerous scale-like small plates. Found in large clumps on intertidal rocks. Often found with mussels on surf-beaten shores.

Giant Barnacle: *Balanus nubilus:*
Diameter to ten cm. Largest of the barnacles. Abundant subtidally, often on pilings in current-swept zones. A variety of animals are found living in large empty shells.
◀

Pelagic Goose Barnacle: *Lepas* ▶
anatifera:
Length to 25 cm. when stalk is extended. Smooth plates. An open water goose barnacle that attaches to floating timbers.

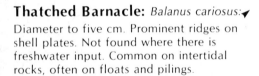

Shrimp and Amphipods: *Phylum Arthropoda:*

Has segmented, hard, external skeleton. Stalked eyes, a pair of jointed antennae and pairs of jointed legs.

Coonstripe Shrimp: *Pandalus danae:*

Body length to 15 cm. Translucent body with red, brown and white markings. Dark irregular stripes on abdomen. Banded legs and antennae. Commonly seen on pilings and breakwaters. ▼

Two Spotted Prawn: *Pandalus* ▲ *platyceros:*

To 20 cm. Large shrimp. Red with distinctive white spots on the first and fifth abdominal segment. Subtidal. Trapped commercially at depth of 30 to 50 m.

▲
Mud Shrimp: *Upogebia pugettensis:*

To ten cm. Grey, brown and bluish body. Equal hairy claws. Often has a small attached clam. Often dug up with clams. Burrows intertidally in mud.

Ghost Shrimp: *Callianassa californiensis:* ▲

To ten cm. Waxy, pale pink and orange body. Large left claw. Burrows in very muddy sand. Often dug up with intertidal clams.

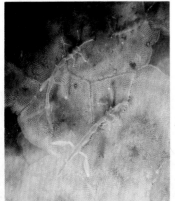

◄ Skeleton Shrimp or Caprellid Amphipod: *Caprella sp.:*

To four cm. Long and slender, resembling a praying mantis. Clings to eelgrass. Often found on hydroids or as shown here, on kelp (encrusted with bryozoans).

Clown Shrimp: *Lebbeus grandimanus:*

To five cm. Translucent body with red and yellow bands and neon blue markings. Found subtidally often at the base of crimson anemones, *Cribrinopsis.*

◄

Kelp Fleas: ►

To one cm. Common intertidally and subtidally, on or under kelp. One species is shown here on the broad kelp, *Costaria.*

Crabs: *Parapleustes pugettensis*

Flattened body with a hard external skeleton or "carapace". May be smooth, hairy or spiny. Often have large claws. First pair of legs often developed as large claws. "True" crabs have five pairs of legs while lithode crabs, hermit crabs, squat lobsters and porcelain crabs have only four pair (including the clawed pair.)

Hairy Shore Crab: *Hemigrapsus* ► *oregonensis:*

To three cm. Square, greyish-green carapace. Legs have conspicuous fringes of hair. Commonly found under rocks in protected intertidal waters.

◄ "Purple" Shore Crab: *Hemigrapsus nudus:*

To four cm. Square carapace. Smooth legs. Often with distinctive spots on the claws but may be green, red-brown or white. Commonly found under intertidal rocks.

Black-Clawed Crab: *Lophopanopeus bellus:* ►

To three cm. Oblong carapace. Color varies from grey to red-brown. Thick, dark claws. Found intertidally under rocks.

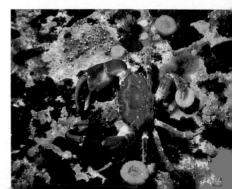

Red Rock Crab: *Cancer productus:*
To 15 cm. across carapace. Brick-red
carapace has distinct marginal "teeth". Black
claws. Young (shown in photo) has a streaked ►
carapace. Found in shallows on rocky shores
and in eelgrass. ▼

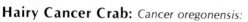

Hairy Cancer Crab: *Cancer oregonensis:* ►
To four cm. Circular carapace. Hairy legs.
Dull red, with black unequal claws. Sits in
small holes, often in empty giant barnacle
shells.

◄ **Dungeness Crab:** *Cancer magister:*
To 30 cm. across carapace. Light brown
carapace; yellow underside. Female has
broad U-shaped abdomen to carry eggs,
while male has sharp V-shaped abdomen.
Found intertidally in eelgrass, often half-
buried in subtidal muddy sand. Trapped
commercially.

◄ **Kelp Crab:** *Pugettia producta:*
To ten cm. One of the spider crabs. Long,
thin legs. Smooth carapace is usually olive,
sometimes dark. Red on underside. Found
clinging to, or around kelp.

Decorator Crab: *Oregonia gracilis:* ►
To five cm. across triangular carapace. Long
and slender legs. Sometimes crab is not
"decorated". Crab actively attaches algae,
sponge and bryozoan to its shell.

38 Crabs

Pea Crab: *Fabia subquadrata:* ►
To two cm. Small, white parasitic crab often found in mussel and horseclams.

Squat Lobster or Galathaeid Crab: ◄ *Munida quadrispina:*
Length to 12 cm. Shrimp-like body with four pair of legs. First pair is very long and with claws. Strictly subtidal.

Hairy Lithode: *Hapalogaster mertensii:* ►
To five cm. across carapace. Hairy body and less flattened. Soft, unsegmented abdomen is flattened rather than folded under. Four pair of legs. Found in shallows under rocks.

Turtle Or Umbrella Crab:
Cryptolithodes typicus:
To 7.5 cm. across. Carapace extends over legs. "Rostrum" between eyes tapers. Has bumps on claws. Variable in color: orange, red, grey, white, mottled. Found intertidally on rocky shores. ►

Turtle Or Umbrella Crab:
Cryptolithodes sitchensis: ▼
To ten cm. "Rostrum" between eyes flares out. Has four pair of legs, the first with smooth claws. (Underside shown in photo).

Puget Sound King Crab: *Lopholithodes mandtii:* ► ▼
To 30 cm. Rough carapace has four prominent bumps. Adults are red, mottled with white and purple. Short blunt spines on four pair of legs. Juveniles are bright red-orange (shown). Found subtidally in rocky areas. (Very different from Alaska King Crab).

Heart Crab: *Phyllolithodes papillosus:* ➤

To 12 cm. All legs with long, blunt-tipped spines. Raised heart shape on back. Mottled green, orange, brown and white. Sometimes found intertidally but usually in rocky subtidal areas.

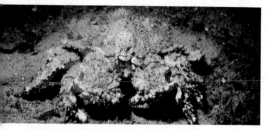

Box Crab: *Lopholithodes foraminatus:* ▲

To 30 cm. Circular cavity formed between first and second legs allows water to pass to gills when the crab buries in the bottom Light brown-orange body. Strictly subtidal on sand-mud bottom.

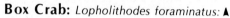

Granular Claw Crab: *Oedignathus* ➤
inermis:

To eight cm. across carapace. Abdomen flattened rather than folded under crab. Olive-brown color. Dark right claw is large and covered with blue "granules". Four pair of legs. Often found in empty giant barnacle shells. Shown on encrusting hydrocoral.

Porcelain Crab: *Petrolisthes eriomerus:* ➤

To two cm. across circular carapace. Brown with blue markings. Often found intertidally under rocks.

◄**Orange Hermit Crab:** *Ellassochirus gilli:*

To five cm. long. Soft coiled abdomen is protected by living in snail shells. Smooth claws and legs are orange-red with occasional white spots. Usually subtidal.

◄**Hairy Hermit Crab:** *Pagurus hirsutiusculus:*

To five cm. long. Soft coiled abdomen that is common to all hermit crabs. Very hairy legs have white or pale blue band. Antennae have light and dark banding. Commonly found intertidally on rocky shores.

Sea Stars:

Central disc with a number of rays, typically five but as many as 40. The size (overall diameter), color and number of rays varies within a species. "Tube feet" with sucker-like tips are used for locomotion, sensory functions, digging, holding or pulling prey. Sea stars can regenerate into a whole individual from one arm! Most sea stars feed on shellfish, some on anemones, sea pens, fishes, tunicates and other sea stars. Sea stars are not edible.

Purple or Ochre Sea Star: ▶

Pisaster ochraceus:

To 30 cm. Five short rays. Short white spines form a pentagon on disc and a distinct pattern on rays. Stiff body. Color variable: yellow, orange, brown, purple or pink. Commonly feeds on mussels and barnacles. Common in tidepools. (small specimen to left)

◀ **Six-Ray Star:** *Leptasterias hexactis:*

To eight cm. Typically six rays. Female broods eggs in a pouch made by arching its disc. Green, grey and sometimes red. Found intertidally feeding on snails and limpets.

Mottled Star: *Evasterias troschelii:* ▶

To 60 cm. Small disc with five, long, slender rays. Numerous spines. Mottled shades of brown, blue and green.

◀**Leather Star:** *Dermasterias imbricata:*

To 25 cm. Five wide rays, soft and smooth. Colors of mottled green, grey and red. Garlic odor. Commonly found intertidally. Can cause swimming response of *Stomphia* anemone.

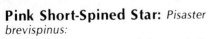

Pink Short-Spined Star: *Pisaster* ▶
brevispinus:

To 45 cm. Small humped disc with five long tapering rays. Spiny surface. Found on subtidal sandy bottom eating clams, sand dollars and other sea stars.

◄ **Sunflower Star:** *Pycnopodia helianthoides:*

To one m. Commonly more than 20 long rays radiating from broad disc. Occasional spines on soft flexible body. Fast moving. Orange, purple to mottled grey. Feeds on clams and other organisms. Common subtidally. Photo shows a sunflower star feeding on abandoned lingcod eggs.

Bat Star: *Patiria miniata:*

To 25 cm. Five triangular rays from broad, thick disc. Rough surface. Orange, brown, grey or black. Found intertidally and subtidally on open coast only. ▼

Striped Sunstar: ▲ *Solaster stimpsoni:*

To 40 cm. Ten to 12 slim tapering rays. Dark stripe on each ray, bordered by blue, pink, red or orange. Often found intertidally.

Morning Sunstar: *Solaster dawsoni:* ►

To 45 cm. Eight to 15 rays from a broad disc. Uniform color: orange, brown or yellow. Eats other sea stars. Shown here eating a leather star.

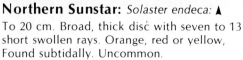

Northern Sunstar: *Solaster endeca:* ▲

To 20 cm. Broad, thick disc with seven to 13 short swollen rays. Orange, red or yellow. Found subtidally. Uncommon.

Long Ray Sea Star: *Stylasterias forreri:* ►

To 45 cm. Five very long, slender rays from a small disc. Very spiny. Brown, dark purple or black. Strictly subtidal.

42 Sea Stars

Blood Star: *Henricia leviuscula:* ►

To 15 cm. Five tapering, cylindrical rays. Blood-red with a yellow underside. Sometimes disc area is light in color (as shown in photo). Often hosts a scale worm.

Painted Star: *Orthasterias koehleri:*

To 38 cm. Humped disc whith five rays. Spiny dorsal surface. Red and purple blotches with white spines. Shown feeding on a clam. ▼

Rose Star: *Crossaster papposus:* ►

To 12 cm. Eight to 14 rays radiating from a large, flat disc. Bristly. Uniform rose occasionally with lighter bands. Related to "Crown of Thorns", *Acanthaster*.

Vermillion Star or Equal Arm Star:

Mediaster aequalis: ►

Diameter to 16 cm. Five rays tapering from disc. "Mail" of uniform, calcareous plates with distinct marginal plates, Red or vermillion. Observed eating sponges and tunicates.

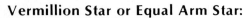

Cookie Star: *Ceramaster patagonicus:*

To ten cm. diameter. Five short triangular rays from a broad disc. Distinct marginal plates. Yellow. Strictly subtidal. ◄

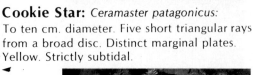

Spiny Star: *Hippasteria spinosa:* ►

To 17 cm. Five rays. Plump body with studding of large, blunt spines. Orange to red. Feeds on sea anemones and sea pens.

Cushion or Slime Star: *Pteraster tesselatus:* ►

To ten cm. Thick disc with five short rays that turn up slightly. Large central opening on disc pulsates. Emits thick mucous for defense. Uniform orange yellow or sometimes radiating color scheme. Feeds on sponges.

◄

Wrinkled Star: *Pteraster militaris:*

To ten cm. Five short, thick rays with wrinkled texture. Large central opening on disc pulsates. Yellow to orange. Observed feeding on sponges.

Mudstar: *Luidia foliolata:* ►

To 30 cm. Five long, tapered rays with spines on edges. Stiff body. Mottled greenish-grey. Found partially buried in mud or sand.

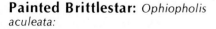

Basketstar: *Gorgonocephalus eucnemis:* ▲

Disc dia. to ten cm. Five rays branch at the disc repeatedly to 12 times. Strictly subtidal. Found in current-swept areas.

Painted Brittlestar: *Ophiopholis aculeata:* ►

Diameter of disc is two cm. Five long, slender rays. Bright red or purplish-red in streaks or blotches. Common in crevices and under rocks. Found world wide.

Sea Cucumbers: *Phylum Echinodermata:*

Round, elongated and soft bodied with numerous fleshy projections. Tube feet are used for locomotion, attachment and some are modified as branching tentacles used for feeding. Feeding tentacles are completely retractable. Detritus is "mopped" up or suspended material trapped for food. Some edible species.

Orange Sea Cucumber: *Cucumaria* ➤ *miniata:*

To 30 cm. Orange body often with brown tube feet. Ten orange to red branched tentacles that trap food. Individual tentacles are inserted and "cleaned off" in mouth. Found between intertidal rocks and on floats.

White Sea Cucumber: *Eupentacta quinquesemita:*

To ten cm. Long, slender tube feet and branched tentacles. Cream color. Often covered by debris. Found between intertidal rocks and on floats. ➤

California Sea Cucumber:

Parastichopus californicus:

To 50 cm. long. Largest of our sea cucumbers. Dark reddish-brown body with large, fleshy, pointed projections. Juveniles may be red. Specialized tentacles that "mop" detritus into mouth. Five internal muscle strips and body wall are edible. Common subtidally. ▼

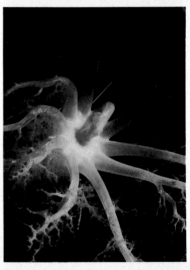

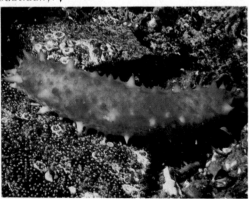

Creeping Pedal Sea Cucumber

Psolus chitonoides:

Rounded body to eight cm. diameter. Resembles a chiton with many overlapping plates. Brilliant red feeding tentacles can be completely retracted. Found on subtidal ➤ rocks.

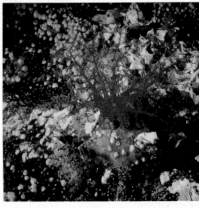

Sand Dollars and Sea Urchins: *Phylum Echinodermata:*

Have internal shell or "test". Long, thin, moveable spines. Long tube feet are used for locomotion and feeding. Sea urchins feed primarily on algae.

Sand Dollar: *Dendraster excentricus:*

Diameter to eight cm. Round, flattened body with fine, short spines. Flower-like impression of five petals on the dark brown test. The white test of a dead sand dollar is often seen on sandy beaches. Found at lowest tides, half-buried in the sand.

Green Sea Urchin: *Strongylocentrotus* ▶ *droebachiensis:*

Diameter of test to nine cm. Pale spines to three cm long. Long, dark tube feet. Common in shallow water feeding on algae.

Purple Sea Urchin: *Strongylocentrotus purpuratus:*

Diameter of test to nine cm. Short, blunt spines to three cm. Dark purple. Found intertidally on rocky exposed shores, often in holes worn in the rock.
▼

Giant Red Sea Urchin:

Strongylocentrotus franciscanus:

Diameter of test to 15 cm. Long spines to eight cm. Bright red, reddish-purple or maroon. Harvested commercially for their roe (eggs). Found in shallows, feeds on algae.
▼

Phylum Chordata

Sea Squirts and Tunicates:

Tunicates are encrusting colonies of distinct individuals in a stiff gelatin-like tunic. Variable in color. Sea squirts have rounded bodies. When disturbed, two rounded siphons appear as crossed folds and squirt water, hence, "sea squirts". The young or "larvae" of both, have a nerve cord and supportive notochord that is lost in later development. No edible species.

Mushroom or Club Tunicate: ➤

Distaplia occidentalis:

Twelve cm. diameter. Forms colonies of club-shaped or mushroom-like masses. Color varies: pale orange, tan, dark, purplish-red. Often found on floats.

◄
Sea Pork: *Aplidium californicum:*
One to 20 cm. diameter. Encrusting rocks, barnacles, shells. Yellow in color. Frequent on outer coast.

Stalked Hairy Sea Squirt: *Boltenia villosa:*
◄
To five cm high. Long tough stalk. Pale orange-brown, hairy, rounded body with two short siphons. Accumulates silts and detritus. Found on rocks, floats and pilings.

Broad Base Sea Squirt: *Cnemidocarpa finmarkiensis:* ▲
To 2.5 cm. high. Smooth tunic is bright, pearly, orange-red. Round apertures close down to little crosses when disturbed.

Ascidia callosa:
Diameter to 7.5 cm. Hemispherical, flattened, smooth, colorless tunic. Common on and under rocks. ▼

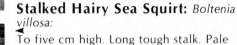

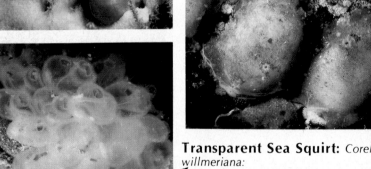

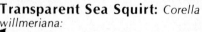

Transparent Sea Squirt: *Corella willmeriana:*
◄
To three cm. high. Glassy tunic. Internal organs visible. Found on floats and rocks.

Horseshoe Sea Squirt: *Chelyosoma productum:* ►

To two cm. Solitary. Short, broad, oval body, firm in texture. Found on rocks and floats.

Wrinkled Sea Squirt: *Pyura haustor:*

To five cm. high. Long siphons. Red-brown, thick, tough and wrinkled "tunic". Found on intertidal rocks. ▼

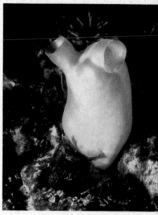

Sea Peach: *Halocynthia aurantium:* ▲

To 15 cm. Smooth, rounded, elongated body with pronounced siphons. Solitary individuals found on subtidal rocks.

◄ **Stalked Sea Squirt:** *Styela montereyensis:*

To 15 cm. Elongated, grooved body thins into stalk. Yellow-brown, orange. Found on rocks in open coast or current-swept areas.

Orange Social Sea Squirts: *Metandrocarpa taylori:*

To two cm. Divides asexually to form numerous rounded individuals that often completely cover intertidal and subtidal ► rocks.

Glassy Sea Squirt: *Ascidia paratropa*

To 15 cm. Translucent, elongated body with many large bumps and prominent siphons. Found on subtidal rocks. ▼

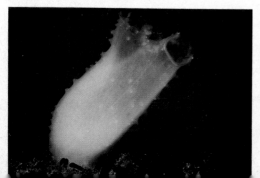

Cartilaginous Fishes

Cartilaginous skeletons as opposed to bony fishes. Includes sharks, rays, and chimaeras (ratfishes).

Ratfish: *Hydrolagus colliei:* ▶

To one m. Long, tapering body with bulky snout. Swims by flapping large fins. Lays eggs in egg case shown in photo. Smooth, grey-brown with white spots. Found subtidally in sandy areas.

Bony Fishes

Have true bones. Range in size, form and habitat. Various examples are given here: sculpins, rockfishes, perch, greenlings, gobes, warbonnets, wolfeels, and flatfishes.

Sculpins

Common bottom dwelling fishes. Stout broad heads with slender bodies. Most have bushy appendages called *cirri* and prominent spines. Abundant in tidepools, intertidally and in shallow water.

Tidepool Sculpin: *Oligocottus maculosus:* ▶

Slender body to nine cm. Variable in color: brown, green or red with five irregular dark saddles on the back. Very abundant in tidepools and intertidally on rocky shores.

Sailfin Sculpin: *Nautichthys* ▲ *oculofasciatus:*

Slender body to 20 cm. Light tan in color with dark patches. A black band on the head runs through the eye. Prominent, tall, sail-like dorsal fin. Found subtidally in narrow crevices. Nocturnal - commonly seen on night dives.

Scaleyhead Sculpin: *Artedius harringtoni:* ▶

Body to ten cm, two pair of prominent bushy cirri on the head of mature males. Variable in color, males and females also differ. Mottled brown, brilliant orange, red and white spots. Common in shallow, subtidal, rocky areas.

Red Irish Lord: *Hemilepidotus hemilipidotus:*
◄

To 50 cm. Single dorsal fin has two, obvious notches. The eyes have numerous flecks. There is a band of large scales four to five wide on the back. Variable color: red or pink with brown, white and black mottling. Because of its cryptic coloration it is often overlooked. Found in rocky areas, intertidally to depth of 50 cm.

Cabezon: *Scorpaenichthys marmoratus:*

To 75 cm. Large, broad head with slender body. Marbled coloration, green-brown and grey. Lays large egg masses in the shallow subtidal zone in winter months. Found in kelp beds and in rocky areas, intertidally to depth of 80 m. A popular sportfish. ▼

Buffalo Sculpin: *Enophrys bison:* ▶

To 30 cm. Large head with slender body. Prominent spines in the head region and raised plates along the lateral line on the side of the body. Variable color: mottled brown, green, pink. Deposits and guards eggs in shallow subtidal waters in winter months.

Grunt Sculpin: *Rhamphocottus richardsoni:*
▶

To eight cm. Short stout body with long snout. Cream body with dark streaks; bright orange on fins and tail. Swims in "hopping" fashion. Common in tidepools and rocky shallows. Often found in empty giant barnacle shells.

Rockfishes:

Many are brilliantly colored: Fins have well developed spines. Found in rocky areas, from the intertidal zone (juveniles are often in tidepools) to great depths. Some species form large schools, others are solitary and hide in crevices. All are edible and many are commercially harvested.

Copper Rockfish: *Sebastes caurinus:* ▶

Length to 55 cm. Light to dark brown with lighter markings. Light colored area along the midline, near the tail. Common in shallow, subtidal, rocky areas.

Quillback Rockfish: *Sebastes maliger:* ➤

To 55 cm. Dark brown with yellow markings and distinct brown spots. White, spiny dorsal fin. Found subtidally in rocky areas. Hides in crevices and holes.

◄

Yelloweye Rockfish:

(formerly *Red Snapper*): *Sebastes ruberrimus:* To 90 cm. Dark orange to red color. Eyes are brilliant yellow. Juveniles appear different, with two light stripes (shown in photo). Found on rocky reefs at 30 m and deeper.

Yellowtail Rockfish: *Sebastes flavidus:*

To 45 cm. Grey-green with dull yellow on fins, and tail. Often have a series of light spots along the back. Often found in large schools, in subtidal rocky areas. ▼

China Rockfish: ▲*Sebastes nebulosus:*

To 40 cm. Black-blue body with broad yellow stripe and yellow mottling. Found on open coast on shallow, subtidal, rocky reefs.

Tiger Rockfish: *Sebastes nigrocinctus:* ➤

To 60 cm. Red or pink body with five black aor dark red vertical bands. Territorial. Often found hiding in crevices in the subtidal zone.

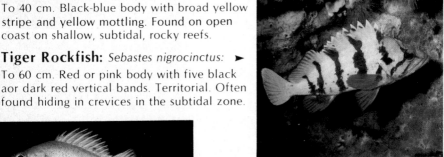

◄**Canary Rockfish:** *Sebastes pinniger:*
To 75 cm. Orange and grey with orange stripes on the head. Schools in deeper water on rocky reefs.

Perch:

Thin oval bodies. Very common schooling in shallow areas, around floats and in kelp beds. Two species are illustrated.

Shiner Perch: *Cymatogaster aggregata:* ►

To 15 cm. Silvery with horizontal, black bars, broken by three vertical yellow bars. Large scales. Abundant. Often found around floats and in sandy areas.

◄

Striped Perch: *Embiotoca lateralis:*

To 40 cm. Dark with many horizontal iridescent blue stripes on the sides. Juveniles often bright golden. Abundant in rocky areas.

Greenlings: Common bottom fishes of shallow subtidal waters, often in kelp beds and rocky areas. They all have a long, continuous, "notched" dorsal fin. A number of greenlings are found in waters between Alaska and California. Three are illustrated here.

Lingcod: *Ophiodon elongatus:* ►

To 1.5 m. Long body with large, broad head. Big mouth has sharp teeth. Typically green to brown with dark spots. Females lay huge egg masses in the upper subtidal zone during the winter months. They are guarded for weeks by the male. Found subtidally in rocky areas, to great depths. Harvested commercially.

Kelp Greenling: *Hexagrammos decagrammus:*

To 53 cm. Male is dark blue-grey with several blue spots on the head. Female is orange-brown with numerous brown spots on the side. Common subtidally in rocky areas. ▼ ►
Eggs (shown below) are guarded by male

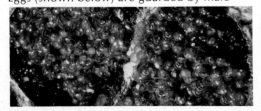

Painted Greenling: *Oxylebius pictus:* ►

To 25 cm. Long, pointed head with bushy growths, "cirri". Tan to grey with approximately seven, dark, vertical bars on the body and fins. Found in subtidal, rock areas.

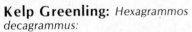
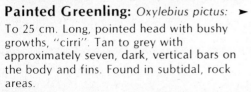

Pricklebacks, Warbonnets and Wolf-eels:

Elongated, eel-like bodies. Often under intertidal rocks and subtidally in rubble, rockpiles and crevices.

Cockscomb Prickleback: *Anoplarchus sp.:* ➤

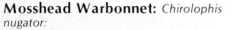

To 15 cm. Fleshy crest on the head. Long slender body variable in color, rarely bright orange, usually dark with a pattern of bars along the back. Often found under intertidal rocks.

Mosshead Warbonnet: *Chirolophis* ➤ *nugator:*

To 12 cm. Dense, short cluster of cirri on the head. Variable color: Brownish with dark and light spots and streaks. About 13 black spots along the dorsal fin. Found subtidally in crevices.

Decorated Warbonnet: *Chirolophis* ➤ *decoratus:*

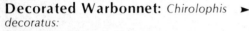
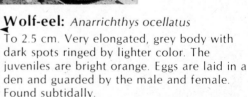

To 40 cm. Large, complex, branching cirri on the head. Long, slender body. Orange-tan with light bars on the side and dark bars on the fins. Found subtidally, usually with head protruding from crevices or sponges.

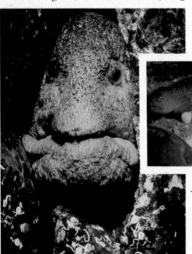

◄ Wolf-eel: *Anarrichthys ocellatus*

To 2.5 cm. Very elongated, grey body with dark spots ringed by lighter color. The juveniles are bright orange. Eggs are laid in a den and guarded by the male and female. Found subtidally.

Flatfishes
Flattened, thin bodies. Popularly called sole, halibut and flounder. Often found in sandy tidepools and subtidally on sand-mud bottoms.

C-O Sole: *Pleuronichthys coenosus*

To 35 cm. Oval, flattened body.
Dark brown to black with an obvious black spot in the middle of the back. Found in shallow, subtidal, sandy areas. ➤

Plants: *Seaweeds:*

Classified according to the colors green, brown and red. They range in size from almost microscopic filmentous seaweeds to the giant kelps. Seaweeds may be thin, broad blades, bushy tufts, or coralline encrustations. Many seaweeds are edible.

Green Seaweed

Typically grass-green or olive green.

Sea Lettuce: *Ulva sp.:* ►

Thin, broad lettuce-like blades to 40 cm. Often perforated. Bright yellowish-green. Found on rocks at the lowest tides.

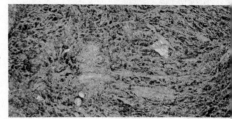

Enteromorpha intestinalis ►

Stringy mats or tufts to 20 cm. long. Yellowish-green to dark green. Found in the upper intertidal zone, attached to rocks.

◄ **Sea Staghorn:** *Codium fragile:*

Repeatedly branches to 40 cm. high. Tubular branches are spongy. Dark green. Common in tidepools and on rocks at the lower intertidal zone.

Brown Seaweed

Typically brown or olive green. Includes the large kelps as well as the common rockweed.

◄ **Rockweed:** *Fucus gardneri:*

To 50 cm. Repeatedly branches. Flexible branches have a mid-rib and swollen tips. Olive-green to yellowish-green. Very common on rocks in the mid-intertidal zone.

Bull Kelp: *Nereocystis leutkeana:*

To 25 cm. long. A long single tubular "stipe"(like a stem) that ends at the surface with a bulbous float with streaming blades. Forms extensive kelp beds at upper subtidal zone.

54 Brown Seaweed

Giant Kelp: *Macrocystis integrefolia:* ►

To 30 m long. Stripe branches to many small floats and blades, ending with split branches. Olive to deep brown. Forms dense kelp beds at the upper subtidal zone in protected waters close to open ocean.

Feather Boa Kelp: *Egregia menziesii:*

To 10 m long. Feathery blades with small floats. Olive green to brown. Found at lowest tides close to open ocean. ▼

Sea Palm: *Postelsia palmaeformis:* ►

Height to 60 cm. Resembles small palm tree. Intertidal in areas exposed to surf. Shown washed up on beach.

Sea Moss: *Endocladia muricata:*

Irregular branching tufts to five cm. Greenish-brown or dark red to black. Found on rocks in the upper intertidal zone. ▼

Red Seaweed

growths, encrusting and erect, branching coralline seaweeds.

Sea Sac: *Halosaccion glandiforme:* ►

Clusters of tubular sacs to 10 cm. high. Reddish purple or yellow to olive brown. Found on rocks in the mid-intertidal zone.

◄

Porphyra perforata:

Thin, iridescent, purple-black blades to one m long. Oily appearance when left dry. Found on rocks in the mid-intertidal zone.

Coralline Seaweed: *Corallina vancouveriensis*:

Long, thin, calcareous, segmented branches to 10 cm. from encrusting base. Deep purple with white tips. Often in tidepools and on subtidal rocks. Shown covered with brooding anemones, *Epiactis*.

Graceful or Tidepool Coral: *Corallina gracilis*:

Feather-like growth to eight cm. Pink, calcareous, segmented branches. Found at lowest tides in tidepools and on rocks exposed to heavy surf.

Coral Leaf Seaweed: *Bossiella sp.*: ▲

Flattened, segmented branches fanning out to 12 cm. from an encrusting base. Pink-purple with white tips. Found on rocks in the lower intertidal and subtidal zones.

Encrusting Coralline Seaweed: ►
Lithothamnion sp.:

Thin, crusty, calcareous patches. Roughly circular shape. Whitish pink to deep purple. Often grazed on by chitons and limpets.

Seed Plants

Rooted aquatic plants. They appear grasslike but are not related to "true" grasses. The plants flower underwater and pollen is carried by water rather than air.

Eelgrass: *Zostera marina*:

Flat, grasslike leaves to 1.5 m length. Dull green. Rooted in mud and sand intertidally and subtidally in protected waters. Important nursery area for fishes and invertebrates. Shown here with herring spawn deposited on leaves.

Surfgrass: *Phyllospadix scouleri*: ►

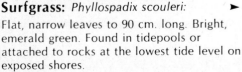

Flat, narrow leaves to 90 cm. long. Bright, emerald green. Found in tidepools or attached to rocks at the lowest tide level on exposed shores.

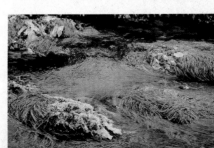

Index

Abalone, Northern, 22
Abietinaria sp., 8
Acanthodoris hudsoni, 26
Acanthodoris nanaimoensis, 26
Acmaea mitra, 24
Adalaria sp., 26
Adocia mollis, 7
Aequorea aequorea, 16
Aglaophenia struthionides, 8
Aldisa sanguinea cooperi, 25
Algae, see Seaweeds
Allopora verilli, 10
    petrograpta, 10
    venusta, 10
Amphipod, Caprellid, 35
Anarrhichthys occelatus, 52
Anemone, Aggregate, 14
    Brooding, 14
    Buried Green, 14
    Crimson, 15
    Giant Green, 14
    Plumose, 13
    Strawberry, 15
    Swimming, 15
    Tube-dwelling, 15
Anisodoris nobilis, 25
Anoplarchus purpurescens, 52
Anthopleura artemisia, 14
    elegantissima, 14
    xanthogrammica, 14
Aphrocallistes vastus, 7
Aplidium californicum, 46
Archidoris montereyensis, 25
    odhneri, 27
Armina californica, 29
Artedius harringtoni, 48
Ascidia callosa, 46
    paratropa, 47
Aurelia aurita, 16
Balanophyllia elegans, 12
Balanus cariosus, 34
    glandula, 34
    nubilus, 34
Bankia setacea, 30
Barnacle, Acorn, 34
    Giant, 34
    Goose, 34
    Pelagic Goose, 34
    Thatched, 34
Batilaria attramentaria, 23
Boltenia villosa, 23
Bossiella sp., 55
Bryozoan, Staghorn, 20
    Kelp Encrusting, 20
    Lacy, 20
    Orange Encrusting, 20
    Spiral, 20
    Bubble Shell, 29
Bugula sp., 20
Cabezon, 49
Caldina luteomarginata, 26
Callianassa californiensis, 35
Calliostoma annulatum, 23
    ligatum, 23
Cancer magister, 37
    oregonensis, 37
    productus, 37
Caryophyllia alaskensis, 12
Ceratostoma foliatum, 22
Ceramaster patagonicus, 42
Chelyosoma productum, 47
Chirolophis decoratus, 52
    nugator, 52
Chiton, Black Leather, 21
    Giant Gumboot, 21
    Lined, 21
    Mossy, 21
Chlamys hastata hericia, 30
    rubida, 30
Clam, Bent Nose, 32
    Butter, 32
    Geoduck, 31

Horse, 31
    Native Littleneck, 32
    Northwest Ugly, 31
    Razor, 32
Clinocardium nuttallii, 32
Cliona celata, 6
Cnememocarpa finmarkiensis, 46
C-O Sole, 52
Cockle, Heart, 32
Codium fragile, 53
Collisella digitalis, 24
Coral, False, 20
    Graceful, 55
    Leaf Seaweed, 55
    Orange Cup, 12
    Soft, 12
    Tan Cup, 12
    Tidepool, 55
Corallina gracilis, 55
    vancouveriensis, 55
Corella wellmeriana, 46
Corynactis californica, 15
Coryphella fusca, 27
    rufibranchialis, 27
    salmonacea, 27
    trilineata, 27
Crab, Black-clawed, 36
    Box, 39
    Decorator, 37
    Dungeness, 37
    Galathaeid, 38
    Granular Claw, 39
    Hairy Cancer, 37
    Hairy Hermit, 39
    Hairy Lithode, 38
    Hairy Shore, 36
    Heart, 39
    Kelp, 37
    Orange Hermit, 39
    Pea, 38
    Porcelain, 39
    Puget Sound King, 38
    Purple Shore, 36
    Red Rock, 37
    Squat Lobster, 38
    Turtle, 38
Crassostrea gigas, 30
Cribrinopsis fernaldi, 15
Crossaster papposus, 42
Cryptochiton stelleri, 21
Cryptolithodes sitchensis, 38
    typicus, 38
Cucumaria miniata, 44
Cucumber, California Sea, 44
    Creeping Pedal Sea, 44
    Orange Sea, 44
    White Sea, 44
Cyanea capillata, 16
Cymatogaster aggregata, 51
Dendraster excentritus, 45
Dendronotus diversicolor, 29
    iris, 28
    dermasterias imbricata, 40
Diaulula sandiegensis, 25
Diodora aspera, 24
Dirona albolineata, 29
    aurantia, 29
Distaplia occidentalis, 46
Dodecaceria fewkesi, 19
Eelgrass, 55
Egregia menziesii, 54
Ellassochirus gilli, 39
Embiotica lateralis, 51
Emplectonema gracile, 18
Endocladia muricata, 54
Enophrys bison, 49
Enteromorpha intestinalis, 52
Entodesma saxicola, 31
Epicatis prolifera, 14
Epizoanthus scotinus, 15
Eudistylia vancouveri, 19
Eupentacta quinquesemita, 44

Evasterias troschelii, 40
Fabia subquadrata, 38
Fusitriton oregonensis, 23
Fucus gardneri, 53
Garvaeia annulata, 8
Gersemia rubiformis, 12
Gonionemus vertens, 16
Gorgonocephalus eucnemis, 43
Greenling, Kelp, 51
    Painted, 51
Halichondria panicea, 6
Haliclona permollis, 6
Haliotis kamtschatkana, 22
Halocynthia aurantium, 47
Halosaccion glandiforme, 54
Halosydna brevisetosa, 19
Haminoea virescens, 29
Hapalogaster mertensii, 38
Hemigrapsus nudas, 36
    oregonensis, 36
Hemilepidotus hemilepidotus, 49
Hinnites giganteus, 30
Henricia leviuscula, 42
Hermissenda crassicornis, 28
Heteropora pacifica, 20
Hexagrammos decagrammus, 51
Hippasteria spinosa, 42
Hydrocorals, Branching, 10
    Encrusting, 10
Hydractinia milleri, 8
Hydroid, Hedgehog, 8
    Orange, 8
    Ostrich Plume, 8
    Pink Mouth, 8
Hydrolagus colliei, 48
Jellyfish, Clinging, 16
    Moon, 16
    Sail, 16
    Water, 16
Katharina tunicata, 21
Kelp, Bull, 53
Kelp crab, 37
Kelp, Feather Boa, 54
Kelp Fleas, 36
Kelp, Giant, 54
Laila cockerelli, 26
Lampshell, 21
Lebbeus grandimanus, 36
Lepas antifera, 34
Leptasterias hexactis, 40
Lettuce, Sea, 53
Leucandra heathi, 7
Leucosolenia eleanor, 6
Limpet, Finger, 24
    Keyhole, 24
    Plate, 24
    Speckled, 24
    Whitecap, 24
Lingcod, 51
Lithode, Hairy, 38
Lithothamnion, 55
Lobster, Squat or
    Galathaeid Crab, 38
Loligo opalescens, 33
Lopholithodes foraminatus, 39
    mandtii, 39
Lophopanopeus bellus, 36
Luidia foliolata, 43
Macoma nasuta, 32
Macrocystis integrefolia, 54
Mediaster aequalis, 42
Medusae, Hydrozoan, 16
Melibe leonina, 29
Membranipora membranacea, 20
Metandrocarpa taylori, 47
Metridium senile, 13
Mopalia muscosa, 21
Munida quadraspina, 38
Mussel, Bay or Blue, 31
    California, 31
Mycale adhaerens, 7
Mytilus californianus, 31

    edulis, 31
Myxilla incrustans, 7
Nautichthys oculofasciatus, 48
Nereis vexillosa, 19
Nereocystis leutkeana, 53
Notoacmea persona, 24
Nudibranch, Alabaster, 29
    Brown Barnacle, 25
    Brown-Spotted, 25
    Bubble Shell, 29
    Common Orange-Spotted, 26
    Common Yellow-Margin, 26
    Giant, 28
    Hooded, 29
    Nanaimo, 26
    Opalescent, 28
    Orange, 29
    Orange Peel, 28
    Orange-Spotted, 26
    Red, 27
    Sea Lemon, 25
    Striped, 29
    White, 27
Octopus dofleini, 33
Octopus, Pacifica, 33
Oedignathus inermis, 39
Oligocottus maculosus, 48
Onchidoris bilamellata, 25
Ophiodon elongatus, 51
Ophiopholis aculeata, 43
Ophlitaspongia pennata, 6
Oregonia gracilis, 37
Orthasterias koehleri, 42
Osteocella septentrionalis, 11
Oxylebius pictus, 51
Oyster, Pacific, 30
Pachycerianthus fimbriatus, 15
Pagurus hirsutiusculus, 39
Pandalus danae, 35
Panopea generosa, 31
    platyceros, 31
Parastochopus californicus, 44
Parapleustes pugettensis, 36
Patiria miniata, 41
Perch, Sea, 47
    Shiner, 51
    Striped, 51
Petrolisthes eriomerus, 39
Phidolopora pacifica, 20
Phyllolithodes papillosus, 39
Phyllospadix scouleri, 55
Pisaster brevispinus, 40
Pleuronichthys coenosus, 52
    ochraceus, 40
Polinices lewisii, 22
Pollicipes polymerus, 34
Porphyra perforata, 54
Postelsia palmaeformis, 54
Prawn, Two Spotted, 53
Prickleback, Cockscomb, 52
Prothothaca staminea, 32
Psolus chitonoides, 44
Pteraster militaris, 43
    tessalatus, 43
Ptilosarcus gurneyi, 11
Pugettia producta, 37
Pycnopodia helianthoides, 41
Pyura haustor, 47
Ratfish, 48
Rhamphocottus richardsoni, 49
Rockfish, Canary, 50
    China, 50
    Copper, 50
    Quillback, 50
    Red Snapper, 50
    Tiger, 50
    Yelloweye, 50
    Yellowtail, 50
Rockweed, 53
Rossia pacifica, 33
Rostanga pulchra, 27
Sand Dollar, 45